W9-AVX-480

MEXICO

Rich in Spirit and Tradition

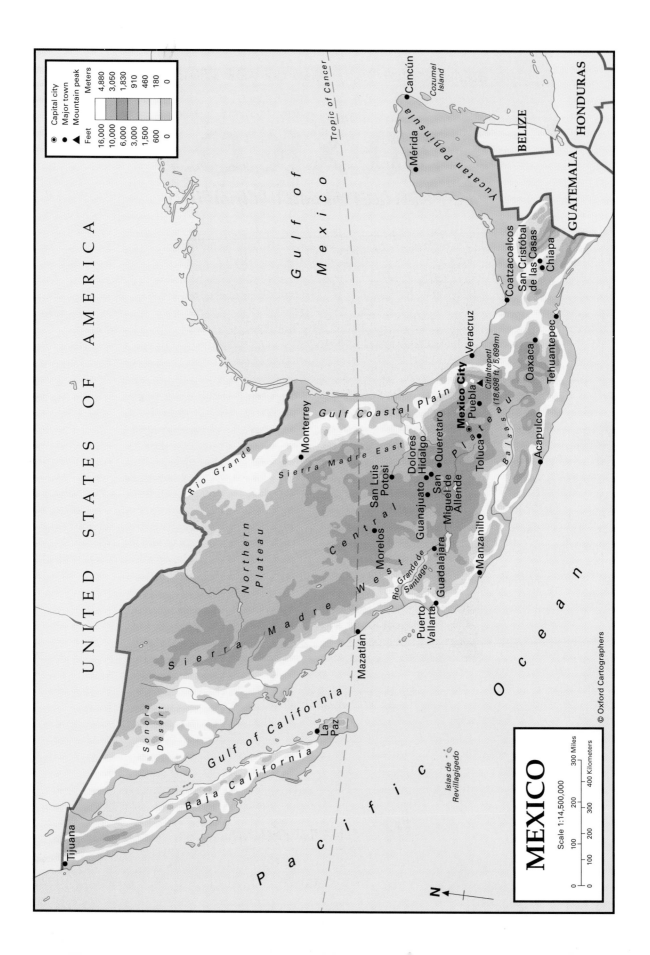

MEXICO

Scale 1:14,500,000

Legend

Capital city	⊙
Major town	●
Mountain peak	▲

Feet	Meters
16,000	4,880
10,000	3,050
6,000	1,830
3,000	910
1,500	460
600	180
0	0

© Oxford Cartographers

Labels on map:

UNITED STATES OF AMERICA

Gulf of Mexico

Pacific Ocean

Tropic of Cancer

BELIZE

GUATEMALA

HONDURAS

Yucatan peninsula

Cozumel Island

Cancún

Mérida

Coatzacoalcos

San Cristóbal de las Casas

Chiapa

Tehuantepec

Oaxaca

Veracruz

Mexico City

Puebla

Citlaltepetl ▲ (18,698 ft / 5,699m)

Toluca

Querétaro

San Miguel de Allende

Dolores Hidalgo

Guanajuato

San Luis Potosi

Monterrey

Sierra Madre East

Gulf Coastal Plain

Rio Grande

Northern Plateau

Central

West

Morelos

Balsas

Pla

Acapulco

Manzanillo

Guadalajara

Rio Grande de Santiago

Puerto Vallarta

Sierra Madre

Sonora Desert

Mazatlán

Gulf of California

Baja California

La Paz

Islas de Revillagigedo

Tijuana

Scale 1:14,500,000

0 100 200 300 Miles

0 100 200 300 400 Kilometers

N

MEXICO

Rich in Spirit and Tradition

Deborah Kent

BENCHMARK BOOKS

MARSHALL CAVENDISH
NEW YORK

10/96

With thanks to Dr. Ruth Borgman of the Institute of Latin American and Iberian Studies, Columbia University, New York City, for her expert reading of the manuscript.

Benchmark Books
Marshall Cavendish Corporation
99 White Plains Road
Tarrytown, New York 10591-9001

© Marshall Cavendish Corporation 1996

All rights reserved. No part of this book may be reproduced or utilized in any form or by any means electronic or mechanical including photocopying, recording, or by any information storage and retrieval system, without permission from the copyright holders.

Library of Congress Cataloging-in-Publication Data

Kent, Deborah, date.
    Mexico / by Deborah Kent.
        p.   cm. — (Exploring cultures of the world)
    Includes bibliographical references and index.
    Summary: Covers the geography, history, people, customs, and the arts of Mexico.
    ISBN 0-7614-0187-3 (lib. bdg.)
    1. Mexico—Civilization—Juvenile literature.   I. Title.   II. Series.
F1210.K46   1996
972—dc20   95-15339

Printed and bound in Italy

Book design by Carol Matsuyama
Photo research by Debbie Needleman

Photo Credits

Front and back covers: courtesy of Robert Frerck/Odyssey Productions/Hillstrom Stock Photo; title page: Norma Morrison/Hillstrom Stock Photo; page 6: The Bettmann Archive; page 9: Tom Till/Hillstrom Stock Photo; pages 11, 13, 24, 28, 43, 57: Robert Frerck/Odyssey Productions/Hillstrom Stock Photo; pages 12, 20, 50 (bottom), 56: Ken Laffal; pages 15, 23: Francis & Donna Caldwell/Affordable Photo Stock; pages 18, 34, 38, 49: David Hiser Photographers/Aspen; page 22: Robert Fried/Hillstrom Stock Photo; pages 26, 30 (bottom), 33, 35, 36: Francis Stoppelman/Hillstrom Stock Photo; pages 30 (top), 54: Cameramann International/Hillstrom Stock Photo; page 40: Micky Jones/Hillstrom Stock Photo; page 45: UPI/Bettmann Newsphotos; pages 47, 48: Nik Wheeler; page 50 (top): Allan Philiba/Hillstrom Stock Photo

Contents

Map of Mexico...Frontispiece

1 GEOGRAPHY AND HISTORY
Mexico, Then and Now...7

2 THE PEOPLE
Who Are the Mexicans?...19

3 FAMILY LIFE, FESTIVALS, AND FOOD
The Mexican Way of Life...31

4 SCHOOL AND RECREATION
Growing Up in Mexico..41

5 THE ARTS
With Hands and Hearts..49

Country Facts...58

Glossary..60

For Further Reading...62

Index...63

Champion of the landless poor during the 1910 revolution, Emiliano Zapata remains one of Mexico's best-loved folk heroes.

1
GEOGRAPHY AND HISTORY

Mexico,
Then and Now

Viva Zapata!

*O*n a clear summer day in 1900 a restless crowd waited beside an empty rodeo ring. People whispered and nudged one another, barely containing their excitement.

Suddenly a horse burst into the ring. A wiry, dark-skinned young man clung to its back as it twisted and leaped into the air. The horse was one of the wildest broncos the crowd had ever seen. But gradually the young rider brought it under control. At last it circled the ring at a smooth, steady canter.

The crowd cheered and shouted, "Viva Emiliano! Long live Emiliano Zapata!"

Emiliano Zapata was born in 1879 in a poor farming village in the Mexican state of Morelos. While he was growing up, a powerful landowner took over most of the farmland belonging to the region's peasants, or campesinos (cahm-peh-SEE-nohs). At that time wealthy landholders were seizing the property of campesinos all over Mexico.

Emiliano's father had to work to raise crops for the landlord. He could keep only a tiny share of the food for himself and his family. When Emiliano was nine years old, the landlord decided he needed more grazing land for his cattle. He took over the last of the campesinos' property and destroyed the little stone chapel where they had worshiped for centuries. Emiliano found his father weeping by the ruins of the little church and demanded to know why the campesinos did not fight back. It was no use, his father told him sadly. The landlord was too strong.

When he reached his teens, Emiliano became a remarkable horseman. He entered rodeos all over Mexico. To the people back home he seemed fearless and heroic. In 1909 the villagers sent Zapata to the governor of Morelos to ask that their land be returned to them. But the governor refused to see him.

When he heard that Zapata had gone to the governor, the landlord threatened to let the campesinos starve to death as punishment. Zapata was outraged by this deep injustice. He concluded that the campesinos would have to fight for their rights.

In 1910 Mexico erupted in a bloody revolution. Zapata gathered a mighty campesino army. Riding a beautiful white horse, he led his soldiers into battle throughout southern Mexico. They reclaimed thousands of acres of land for the campesinos. Zapata inspired his followers when he said, "It is better to die on your feet than to live on your knees."

The landowners were determined to stop Zapata. In 1919 he was ambushed, and his body was riddled with bullets. For years afterward, many campesinos could not believe that their courageous leader was dead. In remote Mexican villages old people still claim they sometimes hear galloping hoofbeats and glimpse a wiry young man on a white horse. They say that Emiliano Zapata rides today.

The Woman with Two Braids

The Mexican poet Octavio Paz once said that his country is like a woman with two long braids. The braids are Mexico's two major mountain chains, the eastern and western Sierra Madre. Between these mountain ranges lies a series of raised, flat areas of land called plateaus. The plateau in the north is largely desert land. The long central plateau, farther south, is more fertile.

On a map Mexico looks a bit like a curved horn, wide at the top and narrow toward the bottom. Near the tip of the horn, the Yucatán (yoo-kuh-TAHN) Peninsula juts into the Atlantic Ocean. A long, narrow peninsula, called Baja (BAH-hah), or Lower, California, dangles from California's southern border. It is separated from the rest of the Mexican mainland by the

Carved by the Urique River, the Copper Canyon in northern Mexico is one of Mexico's natural wonders.

Gulf of California, also known as the Sea of Cortés. Mexico's curving eastern coast embraces a portion of the Atlantic Ocean known as the Gulf of Mexico, or simply, the Gulf.

The Rio Grande, a broad, shallow river, forms much of Mexico's northern border, which it shares with the United States. Mexico's neighbors to the south are the tiny Central American nations of Belize and Guatemala.

From Rain Forests to Cities

At sea level, along Mexico's coasts, the weather is usually hot and humid. On the southern coasts lush tropical rain forests are alive with birds, snakes, and buzzing swarms of insects. In the mountains, however, the temperature drops. There is less rainfall, occurring mostly between June and September. Cactuses grow on Mexico's high plateaus, and goats and donkeys graze on the dry grasses.

Mexico has many extinct volcanoes—volcanoes that have not been active for thousands or even millions of years. But plenty of volcanic activity still seethes beneath the earth's surface. One day in 1943 a farmer was crossing his cornfield in the southern state of Oaxaca (wuh-HAHK-uh). Suddenly the ground felt hot beneath his bare feet. As he fled for safety, the earth split open and a column of scalding lava burst forth. A new volcano, Paricutín (pah-rih-coo-TEEN), appeared overnight. For the next eight years, it spewed lava and ash over the surrounding farms and villages.

If the chickens stop laying eggs and the goats run off into the hills, Mexican farmers grow worried. Farmers know that when animals behave strangely, an earthquake is likely to follow. Minor earth tremors are common in most parts of Mexico. Dishes rattle, bells ring by themselves, and people go on about

A view of the snowcapped volcano Popocatépetl from the city of Puebla. "Popo" was once visible from Mexico City, but is now hidden by smog.

their business. Serious earthquakes can occur, too, destroying property and taking many lives.

Mexico City, the nation's capital, stands in the Valley of Mexico on the central plateau. Some population experts claim that it is the largest city in the world. Downtown Mexico City is a vast landscape of traffic-clogged streets and towering buildings. The city is fringed by sprawling neighborhoods of tiny, huddled houses and narrow, twisting roadways.

Mexico's second largest city is Guadalajara (gwad-uh-luh-HAHR-uh), also in the central plateau. Another important city is Monterrey, a business and industrial center in the north. Veracruz is a major seaport on the Gulf Coast, and Oaxaca is the biggest city in the mountains of the south. Tourists sunbathe on the beaches of Puerto Vallarta, Manzanillo, and

With its glass-and-steel high-rise buildings, downtown Mexico City is a thoroughly modern capital.

Acapulco, resort cities along the Pacific. The island of Cancún was developed as a leading Gulf Coast resort in the 1970s.

Ancient Mexico

The first important civilization to appear in Mexico was that of a people called the Olmecs. Olmec civilization arose in the present-day state of Veracruz around 1500 B.C. and lasted for a thousand years. Little is known about the Olmec way of life. However, these people did leave behind extraordinary carved stone heads, some as high as nine feet.

The most remarkable civilization in ancient Mexico was that of the Maya, who lived in Yucatán and Central America. Maya culture reached its height in the years between A.D. 250 and 900. The Maya built splendid palaces and temples. They carved written messages on stone monuments called stelae. Modern scholars struggled for many years to break the Maya code. Finally, using clues from the Maya language that is still spoken today, they were able to read the ancient writings. Most of them list the names and deeds of long-forgotten rulers.

The Maya were fascinated by the heavens. By studying the movements of the sun and stars, Maya astronomers created the most accurate calendar in the ancient world.

The Aztec Empire

In the 1300s a new culture group settled in the Valley of Mexico on the central plateau. These people, the Aztecs, founded a mighty city that they named Tenochtitlán (tay-nahk-tee-TLAHN). Built on an island in a lake that has since dried up, it was connected to the mainland by a series of raised roads, or causeways. Canoes traveled through the city along canals, much as cars travel city streets today.

The Aztecs built huge temples to their many gods.

Descendants of the Maya stand beside the ruins of the Temple of the Warrior at Chichén Itzá in Yucatán.

According to Aztec beliefs, most of the gods thirsted for human blood. At great festivals, the Aztecs sacrificed thousands of people to keep their gods happy.

Not all of the Aztec gods were bloodthirsty, however. One god, called Quetzalcóatl (kweht-suhl-kuh-WAH-tl), or the feathered serpent, asked only for sacrifices of flowers and butterflies. He commanded his people to be loving and peaceful, but the other gods drove him away. Aztec legend said that Quetzalcóatl disappeared across the sea to the east. But he promised that someday he would return.

The Sword and the Cross

In April 1519, a messenger brought startling news to Tenochtitlán. Strange ships with sails like wings had landed on the Gulf Coast. The men who sailed the ships had pale skin and rode great four-legged beasts.

Montezuma, the Aztec emperor, remembered the legend of Quetzalcóatl. Aztec priests had predicted that Quetzalcóatl would return that very year. Perhaps the leader of the strangers was the god himself.

The pale-skinned men who landed in 1519 were actually Spanish explorers under the leadership of a daring man named Hernán Cortés. They had come to Mexico in search of gold. Montezuma sent them gifts of gold, hoping that they would then go away. But the Spaniards marched 250 miles inland to the Aztec capital. With the help of many small tribes who wanted to see the Aztecs defeated, they finally destroyed Tenochtitlán.

For the next three hundred years, Mexico was under Spanish rule. Upon the ruins of Tenochtitlán, the Spaniards built a new capital, which they called Mexico City. The

Spanish conqueror Hernán Cortés appears as a hunchback in this wall painting by twentieth-century artist Diego Rivera.

Spaniards gave Mexico their language and their architecture. They also brought the Roman Catholic religion. Eager to save souls for Christ, Catholic priests baptized the Indians and taught them Christian beliefs.

As time passed, the people of Mexico grew discontented under the rule of faraway Spain. In 1810 a Catholic priest named Father Miguel Hidalgo y Costilla rang a bell to summon hundreds of Indians to Mass in the town of Dolores. Instead of celebrating Mass, he called for revolution. His army of Indian peasants set out to overthrow the Spanish overlords. Hidalgo was defeated and executed. The war for freedom raged on, however. At last, in 1821, Mexico became an independent nation.

Struggling toward the Future

Independent Mexico was a vast country. It included parts of what is now the United States: Texas, New Mexico, Arizona, Nevada, and Utah, as well as areas of Colorado and California. But few Mexican people lived in this northern territory. Gradually, English-speaking Americans moved into the region, claiming the land for themselves.

In 1836 Texas declared independence from Mexico. Ten years later, U.S. forces invaded Mexico, beginning a war that lasted for the next two years. When the war was over, Mexico had lost all of its territory north of the Rio Grande.

In 1864 the French Emperor Napoleon III drove out Mexico's president, Benito Juárez. He sent a European prince, Maximilian, to rule Mexico. But in 1867 Juárez regained control, and Maximilian was killed.

By the beginning of the twentieth century, rich landholders owned most of Mexico's farmland. The peasants struggled and starved. In 1910 Mexico plunged into a bloody revolution that lasted for seven years. In the south Emiliano Zapata helped the peasants take back much of their land. In the north a series of generals fought for power. When the war finally ended, Mexico adopted a new constitution, calling for fairer distribution of land.

The new constitution permitted any number of political parties, but Mexico did not become a true democracy. It has been under the control of a single party, known as the PRI (Institutional Revolutionary Party), since the late 1920s.

In the years following the revolution, the government founded new schools and hospitals. Highways cut across mountains and deserts. Electricity and running water came to more and more towns and villages. Factories opened in many cities. Millions of people left the land in search of new jobs in industry. Despite all of these changes, however, Mexico is a country in which some people are very rich and many are very, very poor.

In the 1980s new political parties began to challenge the power of the PRI, giving people with differing views the chance to be heard. In their quest for social justice and better opportunities, the Mexican people still struggle to build a true democracy.

MEXICAN GOVERNMENT

The United Mexican States is a federal republic. Mexico's government has three branches, much like the government of the United States of America. The executive branch is the office of the president, the legislative branch is the National Congress, and the judicial branch consists of the court system.

Mexico's president serves one six-year term and cannot be reelected. Mexico has no vice president. If the president dies in office, the Congress must appoint someone to act as president until an election is held.

The National Congress is divided into two houses, a Senate with 64 members and a Chamber of Deputies with 500 members. Senators serve for a term of six years, deputies for three years. They cannot be elected for two terms in a row.

The Supreme Court of Justice is the highest court in the land. The president appoints 21 Supreme Court justices, who serve for life.

For these girls in the state of Hidalgo, just north of Mexico City, going to market is not simply a chore—it's a social outing.

2

THE PEOPLE

Who Are
the Mexicans?

Mexico is the largest Spanish-speaking nation in the world. Yet the land is a rich and sometimes puzzling blend of both Spanish and Indian cultures. It is not always easy to tell who the Mexicans really are.

Spaniards, Indians, and Mestizos

For the three centuries after Cortés conquered Tenochtitlán, the Spaniards controlled Mexico's government, land, and wealth. Mexicans of pure Spanish descent tended to look down on people with Indian blood, treating them as inferiors. After the revolution of 1910, however, Mexicans began to take new pride in their Indian heritage.

Today, about one million Mexicans speak Indian languages that have survived since ancient times. Experts believe that more than three hundred Indian languages are still in use. The most widely spoken of these is Náhuatl (NAH-wah-tl), the language of the Aztecs. About 300,000 people in central Mexico use Náhuatl as their first or only language. Another important Indian language is Maya, with nearly 100,000 speakers in the states of Chiapas and Yucatán. However, most of the Indian languages are disappearing as radio, television, and schools come to the remote villages. In many families the grandparents speak an Indian tongue, the parents understand it and speak a few words, and the children know only Spanish.

Though Mexico's ancient languages are dying out, ancient Indian beliefs are still very much alive. Along with their Christian faith, the Huichol (wee-CHOHL) people of northwestern Mexico believe in the spirit of the deer. The Huichol live by raising corn and beans. They also hunt for game and gather wild fruit and herbs.

Another Mexican people who cling to traditional ways are the Lacandones of the southern rain forests. In addition to

The colonial city of Taxco is noted for its narrow streets, its steep hills, and its exquisite silver jewelry.

farming, the Lacandones hunt, fish, and gather wild fruit as their ancestors did hundreds of years ago.

Mexico's mestizos (meh-STEE-zohz) are people of mixed Spanish and Indian ancestry. The mestizos make up the vast majority of the Mexican population. They live in both rural and urban areas, farming the land or working in offices or factories. Wherever they live, both Spanish and Indian cultures can be seen in their food, festivals, music, and beliefs.

Living in the Country

About one-fourth of all Mexicans live in rural areas, where farming is the chief occupation. Many live and work on large farms, or *ranchos*, belonging to wealthy landowners. Another type of *rancho* is the *ejido* (eh-HEE-doh), in which a group of

THE MEXICAN PEOPLE

Mexicans often remark that "even though there may not be Indian blood in one's veins, it is always present in one's spirit." Actually the vast majority of Mexicans *do* have Indian blood in their veins. About 89 percent of the people of Mexico are mestizos, persons of mixed Spanish and Indian ancestry. Nearly 6 percent are pure Indians, most of whom do not speak Spanish.

People of unmixed Spanish ancestry make up only 4 percent of Mexico's population. Yet northern European looks have long been held to be a standard of beauty in Mexico. Even today, as Indians and mestizos feel a growing pride in their heritage, many of the actors and actresses seen on Mexican television are fair-skinned and blond.

The Maya of tropical Yucatán spend most of their waking hours outdoors. Their homes are simple and small, not much larger than a two-car garage.

families shares the ownership of the land. *Ejido* families work the land together and divide their profits.

Country people, or campesinos, usually live in tiny houses of only one or two rooms. In most parts of Mexico these homes are built of adobe (uh-DOH-bee), a kind of sun-dried brick. Along the coast and in southern Mexico, houses are often made of poles interlaced with reeds or cornstalks. The structure is covered with mud, which dries to form a hard outer shell. There is little room inside for furniture, and people sleep on woven straw mats spread over the dirt floor.

Many rural areas have no electricity, telephone service, or running water. The transistor radio is the only link with the outside world. The radio provides far more than music and news broadcasts. It allows people to communicate with their friends and relatives in other villages. Radio announcers list upcoming weddings and funerals and often pass along personal messages. "Conchita Rodriguez of Rancho Corralejo," an announcer might say, "your Aunt Gloria wants you to come for Sunday dinner at two o'clock."

Along the roads of rural Mexico, burros are still often used for carrying loads.

Traditional fishermen on Lake Pátzcuaro use unique "butterfly nets" to catch whitefish.

The Mexican government has launched a massive program to bring electricity and running water to the villages. Today, television aerials sprout from even the humblest dwellings in communities that were isolated only a few years ago. Children who herd goats on the hillsides all day can now come home to watch reruns of *Gilligan's Island*.

As it was in ancient times, corn is Mexico's main crop. Farmers raise corn for their own use and for the market. Other crops include beans, or frijoles (free-HOH-leez); squash; peppers; and an endless variety of fruit. Most farm families keep a flock of chickens and a few pigs. A donkey is useful for carrying firewood or for hauling buckets of water from the nearest well or stream.

Farming in Mexico is becoming increasingly competitive. The wealthier farmers can afford to buy tractors and other machines that help them work faster and produce bigger crops. It is harder and harder for poor farmers to earn a living. Each year thousands of campesinos leave the land and migrate to the big cities. There they hope to find work, education, and a better life for their children.

Life in the Big City

Not far from Mexico City's airport sprawls a vast neighborhood of tiny, makeshift houses and twisting streets. In the 1950s the crowded settlement did not exist. Today it is home to more than a million people.

Neighborhoods like these have sprung up around Mexico City, Guadalajara, and other major cities throughout Mexico. Most of the people who live there are campesinos who have recently given up farming. They pour into the cities by the thousands and build houses with scrap lumber or sheets of tin or plastic. They are sometimes called "parachutists" because they arrive so suddenly that they seem to drop from the sky.

If they are lucky, the new arrivals may find work in the city's factories, stores, or hotels. Some people set up a sign that advertises their services. A carpenter might display a hammer and nails; a man who repairs shoes might show a sandal and a tool for cutting leather. However, there simply are not enough jobs available for this tide of newcomers and many barely survive by peddling flowers or fruit on the streets.

In contrast with its poor neighborhoods, downtown

Mexico City is a thriving modern capital with high-rise office buildings, apartment houses, and elegant stores and restaurants. In middle-class and wealthy neighborhoods people live in spacious, comfortable homes. Mexican houses in the cities usually do not have yards. Instead most rooms open onto a central courtyard or patio with grass, trees, and flowers. Few families have washing machines, dishwashers, or even vacuum cleaners. Most people who can afford to do so hire servants to help with the housework and cooking.

At the heart of Mexico City lies the Zócalo (ZOH-kuh-loh),

SAY IT IN SPANISH

Buenos días (BWAY-nohs DEE-ahs): Good morning.
Buenas tardes (BWAY-nuhs TAHR-dehs): Good afternoon.
Buenas noches (BWAY-nuhs NOH-chehs): Good evening or Good night.
¿Cómo está usted? (COH-moh es-TAH oo-STEHD): How are you?
Estoy bien. (ehs-TOY bee-EHN): I'm fine.
¡Hóla! (OH-lah): Hi!
¿Qué pasa? (keh PAH-sah): What's going on?
Uno (OO-noh), *dos* (dohs), *tres* (trays), *cuatro* (KUAH-troh), *cinco* (SEEN-coh), *seis* (SEH-ees), *siete* (see-EH-teh), *ocho* (OH-choh), *nueve* (nuh-EH-veh), *diez* (dee-EHZ): One, two, three, four, five, six, seven, eight, nine, ten.

Here is a popular Mexican tongue twister:
Tres tigres tristes comieron trigo de un trigal (trays TEE-grays TREES-tays coh-mee-EH-rahn TREE-goh day oon tree-GAHL): Three sad tigers ate wheat from a wheat bin.

Left: *Newspaper delivery boys make their way through the traffic-clogged streets of Mexico City.*

a large square surrounded by churches and other public buildings. Nearly every city and town in Mexico has some sort of *zócalo*, or central plaza. The plaza is a gathering place during festivals, and a spot where friends can sit on benches and exchange gossip.

Also found in every city and town is the marketplace. Rows of outdoor stalls display pyramids of oranges, mangoes, and melons; slabs of meat; stacks of pottery bowls; and cages of peeping baby chicks. Dresses, woven blankets, and tooled

A dazzling variety of fruits and vegetables is on display at Guadalajara's market.

leather belts hang from racks. In the past, stall-keepers and customers bargained until they agreed upon a price. Bargaining still goes on in some markets, but the practice is slowly disappearing.

The Power of the Church

When Cortés arrived in Tenochtitlán, he brought several Roman Catholic priests, who immediately began to convert the Indians to Christianity. Over the decades that followed, priests worked tirelessly to train the Indians in the Christian faith. Today Mexico is an overwhelmingly Catholic country. Every town has at least one church. The church is not only the community's spiritual hub, it is also a center of social life. The churches sponsor many festivals, which are like huge parties for the whole town. The most important events in a person's life—birth, marriage, and death—are all marked by religious ceremonies.

Religious freedom is guaranteed under the Mexican constitution. Protestants are a tiny but growing religious minority. Missionaries from the Mormon, Pentecostal, and other Protestant churches have won a small but faithful following. Jewish synagogues stand in Mexico City, Guadalajara, and several other large cities.

Above: *For this Guadalajara family, meal-time is a break during the busy day, a chance for everyone to be together.*

During fiestas dancers perform wearing traditional costumes.

3

FAMILY LIFE, FESTIVALS, AND FOOD

The Mexican Way of Life

The people of Mexico usually live near their relatives. A boy growing up in a Mexican village might drop in to see his grandmother after school. He arrives to find his sister and brothers there ahead of him. Soon his aunt and uncle, who live with his grandmother, return home. With them are three of his cousins. While the grown-ups talk, the children run outside to play.

A family in which grandparents, aunts and uncles, and other relatives are deeply involved in one another's lives is called an extended family. The extended family is the basis of daily life in Mexico.

Men, Women, and Children

In general, Mexicans believe that men and women should play very different roles in family life. The man is responsible for earning a living and his word is law in the home. The wife is expected to cook, keep the house clean, and care for the children. This does not mean that the wife is powerless. In many family matters she may have the final say. But she tends to exert her influence quietly, from behind the scenes.

These strict roles are slowly beginning to change. Today women have more opportunities than ever before to receive an education. More and more women are working outside the home. When the mother has a job, an aunt, grandmother, or older sister usually takes care of the smaller children. Mexican parents almost never hire baby-sitters.

Mexican families tend to be larger than families in the United States. By the time they are six or seven years old, children are often taking care of their younger brothers and sisters. Children also help their parents by running errands to the store or the market, washing clothes, and sweeping floors. Children on the *ranchos* weed fields, herd goats, gather firewood, and feed chickens. There is always work to be done, and everyone in the family pitches in.

Holy Days and Holidays

As soon as a Catholic child is born in Mexico, the church becomes a part of his or her life. The child is usually named for a saint. Often the parents choose the saint whose official feast day falls on the date of the child's birth. Many families celebrate saints' days rather than birthdays.

A few days after the newborn arrives, the family carries him or her to church to be baptized. Seven or eight years later, the child will attend First Communion, marking the time when he or she begins to take part fully in church ceremonies. After the First Communion ceremony, the family returns home for a party with cake, music, and gifts.

In addition to these special family occasions, Mexicans celebrate a number of religious holidays. The nine-day festival of Christmas, or *Navidad* (nah-vee-DAHD), recalls the journey

At the Blessing of the Animals festival, priests bless pets and livestock.

OUR LADY OF GUADALUPE

In 1531, only a few years after the Spanish conquest, a recently baptized Indian named Juan Diego met a beautiful lady on a hilltop at the village of Guadalupe Hidalgo. "I am the mother of all of you who dwell in this land," she explained. She told Juan Diego that a church should be built on the spot where she stood. To prove that she was sent by God, she showed him a rosebush on a rocky hill that usually grew nothing but cactus. Juan Diego wrapped some roses in his cape and took them to the bishop in nearby Mexico City.

When the bishop unfolded the cape, he discovered that it bore a painting of the Virgin Mary. The mysterious appearance of the painting seemed to be a miracle. A church was built at Guadalupe Hidalgo, just as the lady requested. To this day Our Lady of Guadalupe is the patron saint of Mexico.

of Joseph and Mary to Bethlehem. The festival ends on Christmas Day, a serious occasion when people go to church and give thanks for the birth of Christ. Children receive their holiday presents on January 6, or Three Kings Day.

The most solemn religious holiday is Good Friday. On this day all church bells fall silent in memory of Christ's death on the cross. On Easter Sunday the bells ring out again in a clamor of joy, celebrating Christ's rebirth, or resurrection.

Saints' days (or, in less traditional families, birthdays) are happy times for everyone. The high point of the celebration is the breaking of a piñata (peen-YAH-tuh). The colorful papier-mâché piñata usually is shaped like an animal or bird. Inside is a pottery jar filled with candy, coins, and inexpensive toys. One after another, children wearing blindfolds try to break the hanging piñata with a stick, to make all the goodies shower to the ground.

Nearly every town in Mexico is named for a Catholic saint, and the towns celebrate their saints' days, too. A typical saint's day festival, or fiesta (fee-EHS-tuh), is held in the town of San Miguel de Allende, near the time of the feast day of St. Michael. Far into the night, people of all ages crowd into San Miguel's plaza. At four in the morning it is time to awaken St. Michael. All the church bells

By tradition, piñatas resemble birds and animals. But they can take any form, even that of Santa Claus.

34

On June 1, the Day of the Mules, children have the chance to dress as grown-ups.

ring at once, people shout and clap their hands, and rockets and fireworks set the sky ablaze. The fiesta continues with performances by dancers called *concheros* (cuhn-CHEHR-ohs), who wear traditional Indian costumes with elaborate feathered headdresses and jingling bells.

Mexico also has several important nonreligious holidays that honor events in the nation's history. Mexican Independence Day, September 16, celebrates the day Father Hidalgo called the Indians to rebel against the Spaniards. The Day of the Race, October 12, honors Columbus's arrival in the New World and the blending of the Spanish and Indian races. Cinco de Mayo (SEEN-coh day MAI-oh), which means "Fifth

Candy skeletons "perform" on the Day of the Dead. Each November 2, Mexicans honor their loved ones who have died. It is not a mournful holiday, but a time of celebration. Children enjoy sugar candies shaped like animals, skulls, and skeletons, and families picnic in the cemeteries.

of May," recalls the Battle of Puebla in 1862, in which Mexico defeated an invading army from France. Like most of Mexico's historical holidays, Cinco de Mayo is celebrated with brass bands, military parades, and long patriotic speeches.

What's Cooking?

Wherever Mexicans gather, whether they are at a public fiesta or a family party, much of the festivity centers around food. Corn is Mexico's main food. It is seldom eaten as corn on the cob, though. Instead the dried kernels are soaked in lime water and ground into a fine meal known as *masa* (MAH-sah). The *masa* is then shaped into flat, round cakes called tortillas (tohr-TEE-yuhz), which are cooked on a griddle.

The tortilla is used in preparing many Mexican dishes. A taco is a tasty treat made by folding a tortilla to hold ground beef, chicken, tomatoes, and lettuce. An enchilada is much like a taco, but it is baked and drenched in a rich sauce of tomato and pepper with melted cheese or meat. Bits of crispy tortilla are a main ingredient in a popular soup, sopa azteca. Tortillas are also eaten alone as a side dish with nearly every meal.

Next to corn in importance is the frijole, or kidney bean. Boiled frijoles can be served alone, they can be mixed with rice, or they can be mashed, fried, and mixed with melted cheese.

Many Americans think that Mexican food is always very spicy. This idea comes from the fact that the chili pepper is often used in Mexican cooking. But there are many kinds of chilis, ranging from mild to blazing hot. The peppers can be stuffed with meat or cheese, as in chiles rellenos. They can be diced and added to a variety of meat and vegetable dishes. Or they can be eaten on the side to add extra zest to a meal.

Each region of Mexico has its own special foods. In the north, cabrito, or baked kid (baby goat), is a specialty. Fish is plentiful along the Gulf and Pacific coasts, and many dishes in the coastal regions are based on seafood. Turkey is enormously popular in Yucatán. Wrapped in leaves (or, more recently, aluminum foil), it is barbecued over stones in a deep pit.

Usually Mexicans eat their main meal at midday. Many businesses close for siesta (see-EHS-tah) between two and four. Siesta is a time for eating and perhaps catching a quick nap.

A typical midday meal, or *comida* (coh-MEE-duh), has several courses. First comes soup, which can be seasoned with a bit of lime juice. Next comes a green salad, followed by a bowl of rice and beans. A favorite main dish is chicken with mole (MOH-lay), a thick, brownish sauce made with peppers,

The ancient practice of making corn tortillas by hand is gradually disappearing. Today, people in cities and towns line up to buy piping hot tortillas fresh from a squealing machine.

onions, almonds, and chocolate. Mole doesn't have a chocolaty taste, but chocolate is indeed one of the ingredients.

The most popular Mexican dessert is flan (FLAHN), a light caramel custard. Flan can be made in many ways. It may be like a pudding, or more like a rich cake. However it's made, it's a delicious end to any meal.

Dressing Up

Just as each region of Mexico has its special foods, it also has its native costumes. However, in most parts of the country, traditional clothing has been replaced by the kind of clothes worn in the United States. Denim jeans are enormously popular in Mexico, as they are around the world.

Despite this modern trend people still wear traditional clothing in Mexico's more remote regions. In parts of the state of Veracruz men wear loose white cotton trousers, embroidered shirts, and colorful woven belts. White cotton is popular in hot regions because it reflects the rays of the sun rather than absorbs them. By wearing white, a person can stay fairly comfortable on a hot day.

The highland Maya of Yucatán's mountains dress to keep warm. Women wear heavy woolen skirts, and men wear thick ponchos, or capes. The clothing of each highland village is decorated with a special design. When two strangers meet, each knows at a glance where the other comes from by the design on his or her clothes.

The most unusual Mexican fashion is worn by the women of Tehuantepec (tuh-WAHNT-uh-pehk) in the far south. They wear elaborate lacy aprons and skirts decorated with gold coins. These coins, handed down from one generation to the next, are the family's fortune. The skirt of a rich woman is extremely heavy. It jingles proudly as she walks, telling the world of her family's prosperity.

In many families everyone works. Even small children can earn a few much-needed pesos.

4
SCHOOL AND RECREATION

Growing Up in Mexico

Nearly half of all Mexicans are children under the age of fifteen. Children can be seen everywhere—at church, at fiestas, selling fruit in the market, waiting on tables in family-owned restaurants. In all of Mexico, adults-only gatherings are almost entirely unknown.

Education Today

On a noisy street in Mexico City the sidewalk is lined with tables. Behind each sits a man or woman with a typewriter. These people are professional scribes. They write letters dictated to them by people who are illiterate—who do not know how to read or write.

Until the second half of the twentieth century, many children from the *ranchos* completed only two or three years of school before they went to work. Others never attended school at all. Today, however, the Mexican government is making a major effort to combat illiteracy. New schools are being built in remote areas. Children are urged to study so they may qualify for better-paying jobs in the future.

Public schools are free for all Mexican children. Many children whose families can afford the cost attend private schools. Most private schools are run by the Catholic Church.

Elementary school, or *primaria* (pree-MAH-ree-uh), extends from first through sixth grade. From seventh through ninth grade, students attend *secundaria* (seh-coon-DAH-ree-uh). By law all students are required to complete *secundaria*, but many still drop out long before they finish ninth grade.

Students who stay in school beyond *secundaria* have two main choices. They can attend a *preparatoria* (preh-pah-rah-TOH-ree-uh), which will prepare them to go to a university. The universities train students for professions such as medicine, dentistry, or the law. Students who do not wish to go to a university can attend a technical school, where they may study subjects such as computer science or engineering. The technical school can train students for a job, or prepare them to go on to a university after graduation.

School Days

Mexican schools are usually built around one or more courtyards or patios. *Primaria* students begin the school day at about 7:30 A.M. Before classes start, the children line up in the main patio and sing the Mexican national anthem. Then they file into their classrooms in a quiet, orderly manner. After third grade all students wear school uniforms every day.

Subjects in *primaria* include reading, math, social studies, science, physical education, and Spanish. By third or fourth grade, most students are also learning the English language. All of the schools in Mexico use the same textbooks. These are paperback workbooks produced by the government.

Classes in Mexican public schools tend to be very large.

In both public and private schools, nearly all Mexican pupils wear uniforms.

Each teacher may have as many as fifty or sixty students. For this reason, most teachers are strict. With so many students, they cannot put up with much misbehavior. If the principal stops by to visit, the children rise politely and say all together, *"Buenos días"* (BWAY-nohs DEE-ahs)—"Good morning."

As they work, the students wait eagerly for the bell to ring, signaling recess. Because the weather is pleasant almost all year, they can nearly always have recess outdoors. In the patio they jump rope, play ball, or run around wildly to burn off energy. All too soon the bell rings again and it is time to file back to class.

Before they go home at the end of the day, all students are expected to help clean up the classroom. Not only do they wipe blackboards and straighten their desks, but they also sweep and mop the floors, empty wastebaskets, and even wash windows. Mexican children are taught that education is a privilege and that they are responsible for keeping their school clean and orderly.

Fun and Games

Every Mexican market has stalls of toys—kites, marbles, and balls; handmade dolls with colorful embroidered skirts; and pottery cups and saucers tiny enough for a mouse's tea party. But compared with American children, Mexican children have few toys to play with. Such toys as Barbie dolls, battery-operated trucks, and Legos are expensive and are not even carried in most stores. Children in Mexico are rarely bored, though. They may not have fancy playthings, but they have brothers and sisters, cousins, and plenty of friends to keep them busy.

The larger towns in Mexico usually have at least one park, equipped with swings, slides, and monkey bars. But the street is the playground for most Mexican children. A stick floating on a puddle can become a pirate ship, and a pile of pebbles can turn into a castle. Girls jump rope, often chanting rhymes handed down by their mothers and grandmothers. Both boys and girls enjoy group games, many of which involve songs and chants.

One children's game popular in and around Mexico City is Doña Blanca (DOHN-yuh BLAHN-kuh). The children form a circle, with a girl playing the princess Doña Blanca in the center, and a boy tries to break through the players' clasped hands to capture the princess. Another favorite game is La Víbora (VEE-boh-ruh) de la Mar, or the Sea Serpent. A long, twisting line of singing children passes through an arch made of clasped hands. The child who gets caught beneath the arch when the song ends is out of the game.

Toward evening, the younger children go inside, and the older boys take over the street. Someone tosses out a soccer ball, and suddenly a game is under way. Pausing now and then to let a car pass by, the boys pursue the ball up and down the block. With shouts and laughter, with sisters and girlfriends cheering from the sidewalk, the game goes on until dark.

Sports to Watch and Play

Soccer, known as *fútbol*—pronounced the same as the English word *football*—is Mexico's national sport and ruling passion. Schools, factories, and civic groups organize teams to play against one another. Children idolize soccer heroes, collecting their pictures and other souvenirs. And every four years Mexico falls prey to World Cup fever. The World Cup competition is a month-long series of matches to decide which nation will be the new international soccer champion. Throughout the World

In 1986 Mexico hosted the World Cup Soccer Competition. For an entire month, the whole nation had World Cup fever.

WINNER TAKE ALL!

Ball games in Mexico date back to ancient times. Archaeologists have found ball courts connected to many ancient Maya temples. Murals on the walls of these courts show that the players had to strike the ball with the heel, ankle, or wrist. The object of the game was to send the ball through a small ring set high on the wall. Apparently the game had some religious meaning that is no longer understood. We do know one thing, however—the stakes of the game were high. The murals in the ball courts make it plain that the captain of the losing team was beheaded.

Cup competition Mexicans seem to talk of nothing but goals and odds and final scores. When Mexico has an especially good team the whole country reaches a state of wild excitement.

Like soccer, baseball and basketball are played by both amateur and professional teams all over Mexico. Mexicans follow American baseball and basketball teams, too.

Every Mexican city has a bullring, or *plaza de toros.* Bullfights—generally in a series of six—are held on Sunday afternoons. To foreign visitors, bullfighting may seem a cruel and gruesome sport. However, fans argue that it is an art that uses bold, graceful moves. The bullfighter lures the angry bull toward him with his red cape, sidestepping just in time to escape the fierce, charging horns. A Mexican bullfight is a spectacle of colorful costumes, thrilling music, and rituals that date back hundreds of years.

Another Mexican sport enjoyed by young and old is jai alai (HI lie). This lightning-fast ball game is played on a three-walled court. The two players each carry a long-handled wicker scoop, which they use to catch the flying ball

Before the matador enters the ring, the picador arouses the bull's anger by plunging long darts into his shoulders.

and send it back to their opponent. Players and ball move nonstop, but betting on the game is even faster. For many people watching at a jai alai match, betting on the players is more than half of the fun.

Mexican pottery is designed to be both practical and pleasing to the eye.

5

With Hands and Hearts

The Mexican people have a deep love of beauty. They fill their homes with flowers and adorn their gardens with singing birds. Many objects such as bowls and baskets, designed for practical purposes, are also works of art. In the fine arts and literature Mexicans have achieved world fame. Music and dance are art forms that everyone can appreciate and in which whole communities can take part.

Clay, Wool, and Straw

Thousands of years ago the Indians of Mexico learned to make bowls and jars from the rich clay they found around lakes and streams. When they put these clay vessels into the fire, the vessels became strong and long lasting. Ever since those

Since ancient times Native Mexican potters have fired their work in deep pits in the ground.

49

ancient times, Mexicans have been making pottery. Every marketplace displays stacks of handmade bowls and platters, cups and saucers, and flowerpots of every shape and size. Mexican pottery is usually painted with flowers or brightly colored geometric designs that vary from region to region. Most pottery is made in small, family-owned workshops. Children learn the craft from their parents and, in turn, pass it on to their own children.

In Mexico's chilly mountains and high plateau regions,

In pottery-making families, the children begin learning the craft at an early age.

Using a traditional spinning wheel, a Mexican woman turns raw wool into yarn for weaving.

people knit heavy woolen shawls called serapes (suh-RAH-pees) to keep out the cold. A serape can cover a bed or be draped over the shoulders and worn as a cloak. Another woven garment, used throughout Mexico, is the rebozo (rih-BOH-zoh), a lightweight shawl of wool or cotton. Indian and mestizo women wrap the rebozo around their shoulders so that it hangs down in front, forming a sturdy pocket. This pocket is handy for carrying things—particularly babies. Many visitors to Mexico remark that Mexican babies seldom cry. Perhaps this is because they are always so close to their mothers, tucked in a rebozo, warm and secure.

The Mexicans use many native reeds and other plants for weaving mats, baskets, and pouches. A *petate* (peh-TAH-teh) is a rectangular mat woven of reeds or palm leaves. *Petates* are used as rugs or sleeping mats. A tough bamboo called *carrizo* (cah-REE-zoh) is woven into strong, round baskets with tight-fitting lids. People from rural areas carry these baskets when they go to the marketplace in town. The baskets can hold lots of fruit and vegetables, and even live chickens. But they are awkward to juggle down the jam-packed aisle of a bus!

Arts and Letters

On the wall of a government building overlooking the Zócalo in Mexico City is a stunning series of paintings. The first scenes show peaceful Indians harvesting corn. Then Spanish conquerors appear with upraised swords. Finally, campesinos march into battle for independence. This wall painting, or mural, is the work of Diego Rivera, one of the most famous artists Mexico has ever produced.

The Maya and Aztecs decorated their walls with paintings. The Spaniards painted religious scenes on the walls of their churches. Thus Mexico's murals spring from both Indian and Spanish traditions. During the twentieth century many Mexican muralists have used their art to carry a political message. Their paintings show the cruelty of the wealthy landholders who oppressed the poor, and the triumph of the campesinos after the 1910 revolution.

Like painting, Mexican literature reaches back to ancient Indian roots. The Maya recorded their legends and history in books called codices. In their eagerness to convert the Indians to Christianity, Spanish priests had most of the codices destroyed. Only four of the original books survive. They give us invaluable information about ancient Maya life and thought.

Aztec poets were held in high regard. They recited their works at festivals and religious ceremonies. Unfortunately they usually did not write their poems down. A few were copied onto paper by the Spaniards, giving us a glimpse into the Aztec world.

During the centuries when Spain ruled Mexico, few women had the chance to get an education. But Juana Inés de la Cruz was hungry for learning. As a girl, she read everything she could find and began to write poetry and plays. Later she became a nun and spent her life in a convent. In every spare moment she continued to write poetry. She often wrote about religion, but many of her poems are about love and the state of the world she knew. Today Sor (Sister) Juana Inés de la Cruz is considered one of Mexico's foremost writers.

During the twentieth century Mexican writers have earned worldwide acclaim. Juan Rulfo wrote stories that drew upon the legends and superstitions of the campesinos. Octavio Paz won the Nobel Prize in literature in 1990. He is best known for his long essay, *The Labyrinth of Solitude,* about the character

AZTEC POETRY

The Aztecs were a warlike people, and much of their poetry was meant to inspire warriors to action. But some of their more thoughtful verses deal with the briefness of human life. This poem is an example:

Ponder this, Eagle and Jaguar knights,
Though you are carved in jade, you will break;
Though you are made of gold, you will crack;
Even though you are a quetzal (keht-SAHL) feather, you will wither.
We are not forever on this earth;
Only for a time are we here.

(From *The Conquest: Montezuma, Cortés, and the Fall of Old Mexico*, by Hugh Thomas. Simon and Schuster, 1993, p. 30.)

of the Mexican people. Carlos Fuentes has written many novels about Mexican politics and society.

Music

When a young man in Mexico wants to impress a woman, he may hire a band of mariachis (mah-ree-AH-cheez) to play for her. A mariachi band usually consists of guitars, violins, and trumpets. Most of the musicians sing as well as play instruments. They perform at weddings or parties, or wander through the town plaza in their colorful costumes, selling songs to passersby.

The accordion is the major instrument in the popular *música norteña* (MOO-see-kah nohr-TAYN-yuh), or northern music, brought to Mexico by immigrants from Germany. Though it can be heard everywhere, it is most popular along the border with the United States and in the northern plateau region. *Norteña* music is sometimes described as the country-and-western sound of Mexico. Singers lament lost love and the hard life of the traveler, or celebrate the joy of fiesta time.

Today American-style rock bands blare out their songs at most Mexican fiestas. But when a religious procession weaves

Most mariachi *bands have six or eight musicians, who wear black suits and distinctive broad-brimmed hats.*

MEXICO IN ARTS AND LETTERS

Sor Juana Inés de la Cruz (1651–1695), outstanding poet and playwright of the Spanish colonial era. Afraid that marriage would prevent her from writing, she became a nun. In her convent she dedicated herself to her poetry, despite harsh opposition from the Catholic Church. According to one story, when her paper and ink were taken from her, she wrote on the walls of her room with her own blood.

José Orozco (oh-ROHS-koh) (1883–1949), considered Mexico's foremost twentieth-century painter. Orozco is one of the "Big Three" mural painters of Mexico. His work shows a deep concern for the rights of the common people.

Diego Rivera (1886–1957), one of Mexico's "Big Three" muralists. Rivera's paintings decorate many university and government buildings in Mexico City. Because of his sympathy with the Communist party, his work stirred up much controversy in the United States.

David Siqueiros (see-KAY-rohs) (1896–1974), the last of the "Big Three" muralists. Siqueiros fought in the 1910 revolution and was jailed several times for his work with Mexican labor unions. His most famous mural, *March of Humanity*, covers fifty thousand square feet of walls in Mexico City and took four years to complete.

Octavio Paz (1914–   ), a leading poet and essayist of the twentieth century. Paz has traveled in Europe and India, but Mexico has been the subject of most of his writing. He was the first Mexican writer to win the prestigious Nobel Prize in literature, in 1990.

through the streets, the marchers follow a more ancient rhythm. The musicians play quavering reed flutes, gourd rattles, and drums made from stalks of bamboo. These instruments have changed little since the days of Cortés and Montezuma. This music from long ago is a living link between the present and the past.

This scene from one of Diego Rivera's murals shows Native Mexicans peacefully at work in the years before the Spanish conquest.

The Baile Folklórico

In the heart of Mexico City stands a white marble building known as the Palace of Fine Arts. The opera company and the symphony orchestra perform in its richly decorated auditorium. But its most popular attraction is the magnificent Baile Folklórico (BA-ee-lay fohlk-LOHR-ee-coh), an internationally recognized troupe of dancers who re-create folk dances from all over Mexico.

Dressed in regional costumes, the dancers bring ancient traditions to life on the stage. They prance and stamp to the lively rhythms of the "Mexican Hat Dance" from the state of Jalisco (huh-LIHS-koh). They perform the *Dance of the Stag* from the canyon country to the north. Their heads adorned with antlers, the dancers move with the grace and strength of deer pursued by swift Indian hunters.

The Baile Folklórico is a glorious pageant that tells the story of a land rich in legend and tradition. It is the story of a people who cherish the old ways while they hunger for change. In Mexico, ancient Indian customs survive beside all the complexities of modern life. The Baile Folklórico offers a glimpse into the dazzling, puzzling, fascinating land that is Mexico today.

Mexico's Baile Folklórico brings the beauty and excitement of traditional dances to audiences around the world.

Country Facts

Official Name: Estados Unidos Mexicanos (United Mexican States)

Capital: Mexico City

Location: Mexico is located in the southern part of North America. It is bordered on the north by the United States, on the south by Guatemala and Belize, with the east coast along the Gulf of Mexico, and the west coast along the Pacific Ocean.

Area: approximately 760,000 square miles (1,968,402 square kilometers)

Elevation: *Highest:* Pico de Orizaba (also called Citlaltépetl), 18,698 feet (5,699 meters). *Lowest:* near Mexicali, 33 feet (10 meters) below sea level.

Climate: subtropical—generally hot and humid—along the southern and southeastern coasts, cooler at higher altitudes. Much of northern Mexico is semidesert, with little rainfall except during the summer months.

Population: 92,202,000. *Distribution:* 71 percent urban, 29 percent rural.

Form of Government: federal republic. In many respects, Mexico's government is modeled upon that of the United States.

Important Products: *Agriculture:* corn, beef cattle, wheat, coffee. *Manufactured goods:* processed foods, motor vehicles, iron and steel. *Minerals:* petroleum, natural gas, silver.

Basic Unit of Money: peso; 1 peso = 100 centavos

Language: Spanish is the official language, used in schools, government, and business. About 6 percent of the people speak one or more of some 300 Indian languages.

Religion: more than 90 percent of all Mexicans are Roman Catholics. About 6 percent practice Indian religions, often blended with Roman Catholicism. There are a small but growing number of Protestants.

Flag: the Mexican flag has three vertical stripes of green, white, and red. Green stands for independence, white for religion, and red for unity. In the center is a picture of an eagle on a cactus, eating a snake. According to legend, the gods told the Aztec people to look for an eagle sitting on a cactus, devouring a serpent, and to build their capital on the spot. The eagle with the serpent is Mexico's national symbol.

National Anthem: *Himno Nacíonal de Mexico* ("National Anthem of Mexico")

Major Holidays: New Year's Day; Three Kings Day, January 6; Good Friday; Easter; Cinco de Mayo, May 5; Mexican Independence Day, September 16; Day of the Race, October 12; Day of the Dead, November 2; Day of the Virgin of Guadalupe, December 12; *Posadas* of Christmas, December 16-25

Flag of Mexico

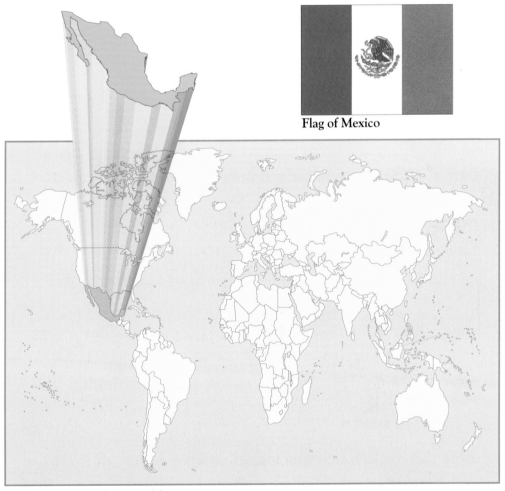

Mexico in the World

Glossary

adobe (uh-DOH-bee): sun-dried brick commonly used for building houses

campesino (cahm-peh-SEE-noh): a person, usually poor, who works the land

carrizo (cah-REE-zoh): bamboo-like reed used for weaving baskets

conchero (cuhn-CHEHR-oh): traditional Indian dancer

ejido (eh-HEE-doh): farmland owned communally by several families

fiesta (fee-EHS-tuh): festival, celebration

flan (FLAHN): caramel custard, a popular Mexican dessert

frijoles (free-HOH-leez): beans

jai alai (HI lie): popular game somewhat resembling tennis

masa (MAH-sah): flour used for making corn tortillas

mestizo (meh-STEE-zoh): a person of mixed Indian and Spanish ancestry

mole (MOH-lay): rich sauce made with a variety of ingredients, including almonds, chili, and chocolate

piñata (peen-YAH-tuh): clay jar decorated to resemble an animal and filled with candy, to be broken by the children during a fiesta

petate (peh-TAH-teh): mat woven of straw or reeds

posada (puh-SAH-duh): inn; Christmas party at which guests reenact the story of Mary and Joseph searching for an inn in Bethlehem

rebozo (rih-BOH-zoh): woven shawl worn by women, usually draped over the shoulders to form a pouch for carrying a baby

serape (suh-RAH-pee): heavy woolen shawl, worn as a cloak or used as a blanket

sombrero (suhm-BREHR-roh): broad-brimmed hat of felt or straw

tortilla (tohr-TEE-yuh): flat, round bread

For Further Reading

Ancona, George. *Pablo Remembers*. New York: Lathrop, 1993.

Bains, Rae. *Benito Juarez: Hero of Modern Mexico*. Mahwah, New Jersey: Troll, 1992.

Barysh, Ann. *The Suitcase Scholar Goes to Mexico*. New York: Lerner, 1992.

Fisher, Leonard E. *Pyramid of the Sun, Pyramid of the Moon*. New York: Macmillan, 1988.

Flint, David. *Mexico*. New York: Raintree, 1993.

Gollub, Matthew. *The Moon Was a Fiesta*. (fiction) New York: Morrow, 1994.

Howard, John. *Mexico*. Morristown, New Jersey: Silver Burdett, 1992.

Reilly, Mary Jo. *Mexico*. New York: Marshall Cavendish, 1993.

Silverthorn, Elizabeth. *Fiesta: Mexico's Great Celebrations*. Brookfield, Connecticut: Millbrook, 1992.

Stein, R. Conrad. *The Mexican Revolution, 1910–1920*. New York: New Discovery, Macmillan, 1994.

Strasser, Todd. *The Diving Bell*. (fiction) New York: Scholastic, 1992.

Index

Page numbers for illustrations are in boldface

Americans, 16
animals, 10, **23,** 24–25, **33**
arts, **48, 49,** 49–52
Aztecs, 13–14, 19, 51–53

Baile Folklórico, 57, **57**
Baja California, 9
beaches, 11–12
bicycles, **26**
bullfights, 46, **47**
burros, **23**

campesinos (farmers), 22–25, 51–52
    revolution of, 7–8, 16
Cancún, 12
Catholic Church, 15, 29, 32–35, 42
children, 41–43, 44–47, 51
    jobs of, 32, **40,** 41, 50, **50**
cities, 11, **20–21,** 25–29
clothing, 38–39, **43,** 50–51
    of dancers, **30,** 35
constitution, Mexican, 16
corn, 24, 26–37, **38,** 51
Cortés, Hernán, 14, 15, 29
Cruz, Juana Inés de la, 52, 55

dance, **30,** 35, 49, 57

earthquakes, 10–11
economy, 17
education, 32, 41–43, **43**
electricity, 23–24

families, **30,** 31–32, **36, 40, 50**
farming, 21–22, 24–25
fiestas, **30.** *See also* holidays
fishing, **24**
foods, 20–21, 36–38, **38**
Fuentes, Carlos, 53

games, 44–47
geography, 8–10, 16
government, 16–17, 24, 41
Guadalajara, 11, 25, **28,** 29
Gulf of Mexico, 9–10

Hidalgo y Costilla, Father Miguel, 15
holidays, 32–35, **33–36**
homes, **22,** 22–24, 25–27

Indians, 12–15, 19–21, **56**

jobs, 17, 25, 31–32, **40**

Lacandones, 20–21
landlords, 7–8, 16, 21, 51–52
languages, 12, 19, 27, 42
literature, 52–53, 55

mariachis, 53, **54**
markets, **18,** 28–29, 44
Maya, 12, **13, 22,** 39, 46, 51–52
    language of, 19–20
meals, **30,** 37–38
mestizos, 21
Mexican-American War, 16
Mexican Independence Day, 35
Mexico City, 11, **12,** 14, 25–28, **26,** 29, 41, 44, 51, 55
money, 17, 39, **40**
music, 49, 53–55, **54**

National Congress, 17
norteña music, 53–54

Oaxaca, 10, 11
Olmecs, 12
Orozco, José, 55

paintings, 51–52, 55
Paz, Octavio, 8, 52–53, 55

plazas, 27–28
politics, 16–17, 52, 55
pottery, **48, 49,** 49–50, **50**
president, 17

Quetzalcóatl, 14

rain forests, 10
religions, 29, 32–36, 54–55
    Indian, 14, 20
revolution, Mexican, 8, 15, 16, 35
    art of, 51–52
Rio Grande, 10
Rivera, Diego, **15,** 51, 55, **56**
Rulfo, Juan, 52

schools. *See* education
Siqueiros, David, 55
soccer, 44–46, **45**
Spaniards, 14, 19, 21, 51–52
spinning, **50,** 51
sports, 44–47
Supreme Court of Justice, 17

Taxco, **20–21**
Temple of the Warrior, **13**
temples, 13–14, 46
Tenochtitlán, 13, 14, 19, 29
territory, Mexican, 16
transportation, **23, 26**

Valley of Mexico, 13
Veracruz, 11, 39
villages, 22–24
volcanoes, 10

weather, 10
World Cup competition, **45,** 45–46

Yucatán Peninsula, 9, 12

Zapata, Emiliano, **6,** 7–8, 16

About the Author

Deborah Kent grew up in Little Falls, New Jersey, and received her B.A. degree from Oberlin College. Before launching her writing career, she did social work in New York City and helped start a school for disabled children in San Miguel de Allende, Mexico. She continues to visit the town for several weeks each year. Ms. Kent has written more than a dozen young-adult novels, as well as numerous nonfiction books for children. She lives in Chicago with her husband, children's book author R. Conrad Stein, and their daughter, Janna.